By Shelly Nielsen
Illustrated by Anastasia Mitchell

Published by Abdo & Daughters, 4940 Viking Drive Suite 622, Edina, Minnesota 55435.

Library bound edition distributed by Rockbottom Books, Pentagon Tower, P.O. Box 36036, Minneapolis, Minnesota 55435.

Edited by Julie Berg

LIBRARY OF CONGRESS CATALOGING-IN-PUBLICATION DATA
Nielsen, Shelly. 1958 -
    I love water / written by Shelly Neilsen : [edited by Julie Berg].
       p.   cm. -- (Target Earth)
    Summary: Brief text and suggested activities introduce water an essential part of our world.
    ISBN 1-56239-190-9
    1. Water -- Juvenile literature. [1. Water.] I. Berg, Julie. II. Title.   III. Series.
    GB662.3.N54   1993
    553.7--dc20
    [B]   93-18957
                                    CIP
                                    AC

 Thanks To The Trees From Which This Recycled Paper Was First Made.

I promise to love the water. I'll keep it clean, like I ought to. I'll let it splash my bare legs or drink it down in great big gulps. I'm glad I'm a kid who loves water.

Slosh, **slosh**, **slosh**. There's water everywhere
I look! Clear water. Deep water. Cold water.
Hot water. I love water.

I LOVE WATER IDEA BOX

What's more delicious than a cold glass of water on a hot day? Have you ever tasted purple water? Add a drop of red food coloring to a glass of water. Now add a drop of blue. Stir, add an ice cube, and sip. Ah! No matter the color, clean water is delicious!

I love water. Watch me hook a garden hose to the sprinkler and turn it on. Do I dare run through? One, two, three—go! Eeek! It's cold! I love water.

I LOVE WATER
♥ IDEA BOX ♥

Have a water parade.
Put on your bathing
suit and call some
friends. Ask them
to bring squirt toys.
Single file, everyone.
Ready?   Forward,
march!

I love water. All I need is water and bubble bath
to make piles of suds. Hills of suds. Mountains
of suds. Look out! Stand back! It's the Suds
Monster! I love water.

I LOVE WATER
IDEA BOX

Have your mom or dad hide small toys in the bathtub. Then add your bubble bath and water. During your bath, search for the toy treasures. How many can you find?

I love water—and I'm not the only one. All day long my goldfish swim in their bowl. They swish their tails and always keep their eyes open under water. I love water.

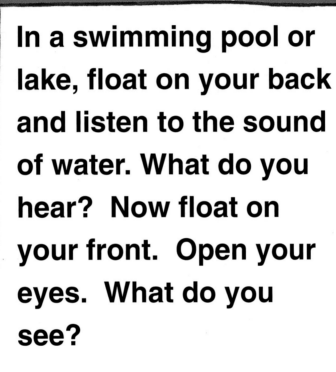

I LOVE WATER IDEA BOX

In a swimming pool or lake, float on your back and listen to the sound of water. What do you hear? Now float on your front. Open your eyes. What do you see?

I love water—especially rain. Watch it sprinkle!
I open my mouth and catch a drop...or two...or
three. The thirsty plants like rain, too. I love
water.

I LOVE WATER IDEA BOX

Make this craft on a rainy day. First, fill a clean jar with water—not quite to the top. Add a drop or two of dishwashing liquid. Sprinkle in some glitter. Close it tight, and shake. It's raining! Glue a round piece of felt or colored paper to the lid and add a ribbon border, if you wish.

I love water. Splish, splash, I'm giving the car a bath. Squirt, squirt, look out dirt! The water runs down the gutter and, suddenly, the car is shiny-clean! I love water.

Get some friends together.
Give everyone a paper cup.
Fill yours to the brim with
water. Stand at the front of
the line.   At the signal
"go," pour your water into
the next player's cup. How
fast can your friends pour
the water from cup to cup?
How much water is left at
the end of the line? Play
the game again, only faster.

I love water. Waterfalls are wonderful, but there's only one way to catch one. Do you have a camera? Aim and shoot. I love water.

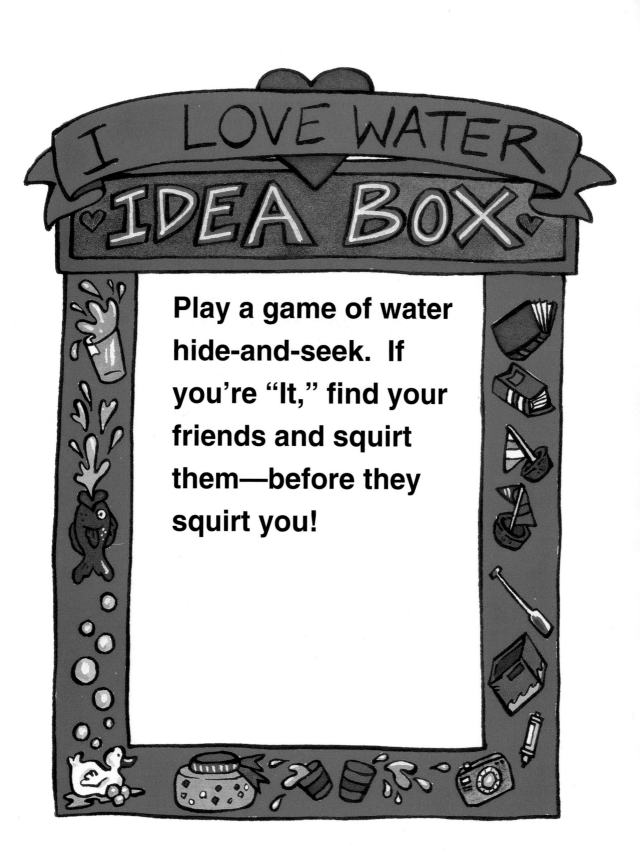

I LOVE WATER
IDEA BOX

Play a game of water hide-and-seek. If you're "It," find your friends and squirt them—before they squirt you!

I love water. Go ahead, ocean—roar! And I'll
yell, too. First, you chase me. Then I'll chase
you. I love water.

I LOVE WATER
IDEA BOX

Find a large box. Climb inside. Imagine what it would be like to be the captain of a boat on the ocean. Can you feel the waves rocking? Decorate your boat with paints.

I love water. After I play outside, it washes my clothes clean. It washes me, too—with a little help from Mom. I love water.

Make a boat to float in the bathtub or sink. Crack a walnut in half. Roll a small ball of clay and press it into the bottom of the shell. Cut a tiny sail from paper. Poke the toothpick through the sail. Push the toothpick into the clay. Happy sailing, captain!

I love water—clean, clear water. Who will keep
the Earth's water clean? I will, because I love
water.

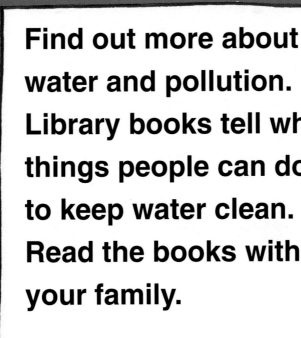

I LOVE WATER IDEA BOX

Find out more about water and pollution. Library books tell what things people can do to keep water clean. Read the books with your family.

TARGET EARTH™ COMMITMENT

At Target, we're committed to the environment. We show this commitment not only through our own internal efforts but also through the programs we sponsor in the communities where we do business.

Our commitment to children and the environment began when we became the Founding International Sponsor for Kids for Saving Earth, a non-profit environmental organization for kids. We helped launch the program in 1989 and supported its growth to three-quarters of a million club members in just three years.

Our commitment to children's environmental education led to the development of an environmental curriculum called Target Earth™, aimed at getting kids involved in their education and in their world.

In addition, we worked with Abdo & Daughters Publishing to develop the Target Earth™ Earthmobile, an environmental science library on wheels that can be used in libraries, or rolled from classroom to classroom.

Target believes that the children are our future and the future of our planet. Through education, they will save the world!

TARGET®

Minneapolis-based Target Stores is an upscale discount department store chain of 517 stores in 33 states coast-to-coast, and is the largest division of Dayton Hudson Corporation, one of the nation's leading retailers.